Kids Living Green

Let's Recycle!

by Jenna Lee Gleisner

Bullfrog Books

Ideas for Parents and Teachers

Bullfrog Books let children practice reading informational text at the earliest reading levels. Repetition, familiar words, and photo labels support early readers.

Before Reading

- Discuss the cover photo. What does it tell them?

- Look at the picture glossary together. Read and discuss the words.

Read the Book

- "Walk" through the book and look at the photos. Let the child ask questions. Point out the photo labels.

- Read the book to the child, or have him or her read independently.

After Reading

- Prompt the child to think more. Ask: There are ideas for reusing and recycling in this book. What other ways can you think of?

Bullfrog Books are published by Jump!
5357 Penn Avenue South
Minneapolis, MN 55419
www.jumplibrary.com

Library of Congress Cataloging-in-Publication Data

Names: Gleisner, Jenna Lee, author.
Title: Let's recycle! / by Jenna Lee Gleisner.
Description: Minneapolis, MN: Jump!, Inc., [2019]
Series: Let's recycle!
Audience: Age 5-8. | Audience: K to grade 3.
Includes bibliographical references and index.
Identifiers: LCCN 2018034822 (print)
LCCN 2018036744 (ebook)
ISBN 9781641284554 (e-book)
ISBN 9781641284530 (hardcover : alk. paper)
ISBN 9781641284547 (pbk.)
Subjects: LCSH: Recycling (Waste, etc.)
Juvenile literature.
Classification: LCC TD794.5 (ebook)
LCC TD794.5 .G57 2019 (print) | DDC 363.72/82—dc23
LC record available at https://lccn.loc.gov/2018034822

Editor: Susanne Bushman
Designer: Molly Ballanger

Photo Credits: YinYang/iStock, cover; Rawpixel. com/Shutterstock, 1; DecNui/iStock, 3; kanvag/ Shutterstock, 4; Wavebreakmedia/iStock, 5; KatarzynaBialasiewicz/iStock, 6–7, 23bl; JIANG HONGYAN/Shutterstock, 8; aykuterd/iStock, 8–9; LoyFah4158/Shutterstock, 10–11; Natalia van D/ Shutterstock, 12; terra24/iStock, 13, 23tl; JAJMO/ iStock, 14–15, 23br; wavebreakmedia/Shutterstock, 16 (child); Mega Pixel/Shutterstock, 16 (tote); Janine Lamontagne/iStock, 17; Steve Debenport/iStock, 18–19; Michael Tatman/Shutterstock, 20–21; kosam/ Shutterstock, 22 (left); photosync/Shutterstock, 22 (center); Hortimages/Shutterstock, 22 (right); zhangyang13576997233/Shutterstock, 23tr; Tom Merton/Shutterstock, 24.

Printed in the United States of America at Corporate Graphics in North Mankato, Minnesota.

Table of Contents

Reuse

This is garbage.

It piles up.

We can help keep Earth clean.

How?

Let's recycle!

PAPER

GLASS

We sort.

Paper. Glass. And more!

Into what?

Bins.

ALUMINUM

They are made into
new things.

This saves energy.

recycled
plastic

9

We reuse.

We use both
sides of paper.

This saves trees.

food
scraps

We save food scraps.
Why?
To make compost.

We put it on soil.

It helps plants grow.

compost

13

water
bottle

Luke has a water bottle.

He reuses it.

This saves bottles.

Mia uses a tote.

Where?

The library.

tote

And the store!

This saves bags.

Gia gives away her old toys.

She does not throw them away.

old tire

Can you reuse?

Yes!

How will you do it?

Let's Do It!

Repurpose a Jar

One way to recycle is to repurpose something. This means to use it again but in a different way. Do you have old things you don't need or use anymore? Maybe clothes. Or towels. Or glass jars. You can make them into something new!

Picture Glossary

compost
Organic materials, such as fruit and vegetable scraps, that are added to soil to make it more productive.

energy
Power from coal, electricity, or other sources that makes machines work and produces heat.

recycle
To process old items, such as glass, plastic, paper, aluminum, and tin cans, into new products.

reuse
To use again.

Index

To Learn More

Finding more information is as easy as 1, 2, 3.

❶ Go to www.factsurfer.com

❷ Enter "let'srecycle!" into the search box.

❸ Click the "Surf" button to see a list of websites.

24